BRITAIN IN OLD PH

Ladywood Revisited

NORMAN BARTLAM

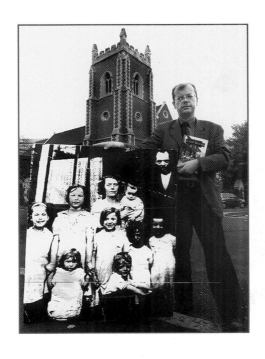

SUTTON PUBLISHING

Sutton Publishing Limited
Phoenix Mill · Thrupp · Stroud
Gloucestershire · GL5 2BU

First published 2001

Reprinted in 2001

Cover photographs: *front*: New Spring Street from the corner of Icknield Street, August 1968. *Back*: Staff from the canteen of Wiggins' in Wiggin Street at the Tower Ballroom with friends and partners, *c.* 1956. *Title page photograph*: Courtesy of *Birmingham Evening Mail*.

British Library Cataloguing in Publication Data
A catalogue record for this book is available from the British Library.

ISBN 0-7509-2745-3

Typeset in 10.5/13.5 Photina.
Typesetting and origination by Sutton Publishing Limited.
Printed and bound in England by J.H. Haynes & Co. Ltd, Sparkford.

ST JOHN'S CHURCH, LADYWOOD: THE ARTS AND EDUCATION DEVELOPMENT PROJECT

St John's Church, built 1852–4, is a powerful symbol of continuity and Christian faith throughout the changing times recorded in this fascinating book.

The exterior of the church building was restored in 1998/9 with the support of the Heritage Lottery Fund. Inside, it offers great potential with its fine space and acoustics. Plans are underway for an Arts and Education programme to incorporate performances of music, drama and dance, exhibitions of art and religious education. St John's will continue to be the centre of Anglican worship in Ladywood. In partnership with the community – including the local Buddhists – it will become a creative meeting-place welcoming all-comers: a modern expression of the spirit of Ladywood for 2001.

Large-scale funds are required to modernise the interior for such purposes, through improvements to lighting, seating, heating and catering.

St John's appreciates Norman Bartlam's generosity in donating to St John's a percentage of his royalties from the sale of this book.

Appeal Director: the Revd Richard Tetlow, St John's Vicarage, Darnley Road, Ladywood, Birmingham, B16 8TF

CONTENTS

The Heart family, Osler Street, in 1927.

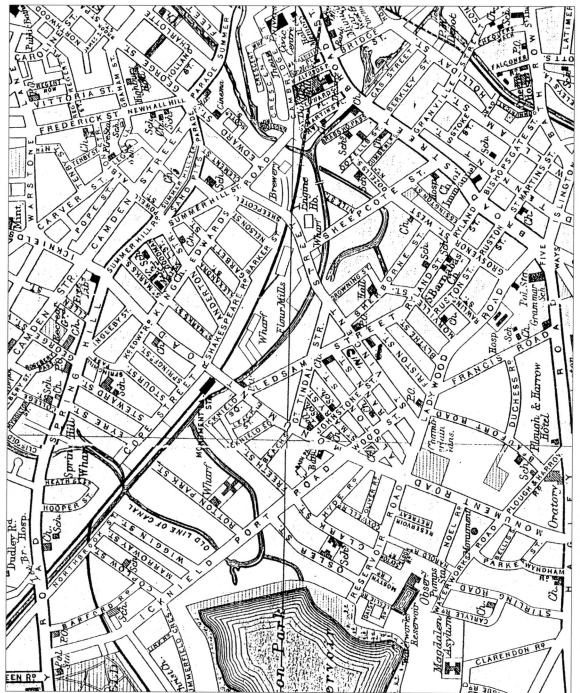

A map of Ladywood as it looked in 1947.

INTRODUCTION & ACKNOWLEDGEMENTS

When my first book, *Britain in Old Photographs: Ladywood*, was published in 1999 there was a great response from people who eagerly read and looked through its pages. Two frequently asked questions were: 'How old does something have to be in order to be old enough to be in the book?' and 'Where does Ladywood begin and end?'

There is no straightforward answer to either question! Anything that has happened is history and can therefore be included. Even some of the post-1960s buildings have been closed or demolished. An eight year old recently said to me that her dad had said Ladywood once had a swimming baths. Older people would remember the large Victorian building, but she was referring to the baths it replaced in 1940 which was demolished a few years ago. Both buildings are part of Ladywood's rich history and photographs of them are included in this book.

Ladywood School, which closed in 1990, is as much part of the history of Ladywood as the school it replaced on Osler Street. Osler Street School, of course, has the longer history, and it is featured in this book along with the primary schools. How many thousands of children went through their school years in Ladywood and have 'sir stificates' to prove it!

One thing that is more important to Ladywood than bricks and mortar is the people. This book has a remarkable collection of photographs taken from the albums (and biscuit tins) of many 'ordinary' Ladywood people. These illustrate how the community has changed over the years – from back-to-back houses with tin bath on the wall to blocks of flats and newer apartments, from corner shops to Tesco and from the fleapits and pubs where the 'owlman' supped 'arfamoild' to the restaurants and multi-screen cinemas due to open on the site of the Children's Hospital. In short, everything changed and is changing again, so anything you can remember, and more importantly have a photograph of, is included in this book. It is important to include not just the photographs and simple captions but also a few quotes that encapsulate the memories that the photographs bring back. This makes the book so much more than just a collection of pictures.

As for the question about where does Ladywood begin and end, well if you asked ten different people you would probably get ten different answers! The road sign for Ladywood swung from a post which was outside the Freeth Arms on Icknield Port Road near Freeth Street, which means that if the signs are to be believed The Crown was outside Ladywood. Most people would disagree with that. How far do you have to go up Icknield Port Road before you leave Ladywood and enter Winson Green? Just to confuse things the Rezza is officially called Edgbaston Reservoir. For me, Ladywood includes the streets which contained the great industrial premises such as McKechnie's and Docker's, but many people only went up to the top of Icknield Port Road when they were being carried to the workhouse!

Older people will recall that Spring Hill and nearby Brookfields once had separate identities. Today most people would regard them as Ladywood. The name Spring Hill is dying out; if the library were to be demolished then the name would disappear altogether. The name Brookfields is in more danger of disappearing. The shopping centre bears the name Brookfields but when that is demolished the name will have almost certainly been lost, although Brookfields School still exists in spite of Hitler's efforts. Summerhill and Sandpits are two more names that are fading away. These areas are included in this book.

Is the area around the International Convention Centre in Ladywood? Today the ICC and Brindleyplace work hard to include the people of Ladywood in their activities. In days gone by the canals and industrial premises, such as those on Sheepcote Street and Oozells Street, employed thousands of Ladywood people. Many people regarded Bingley Hall and St Peter's Church and school as 'part of us'. Perhaps Broad Street forms a natural boundary for Ladywood. The other side of the street is in Bath Row, as it was once called, or, as the planners later called it, Lee Bank. Today part of it is now called Attwood Green!

From Five Ways, Hagley Road perhaps forms a boundary. Certainly, the upmarket Gough-Calthorpe inspired developments belong to Edgbaston, but on the Ladywood side of the road towards the Ivy Bush and the Oratory there were, and still are, some high-class developments, and large houses still exist on the Ivy Bush end of Monument Road. According to the district sign these buildings are not in Ladywood: the Ladywood sign is near to the junction with Reservoir Road. This area is, however, included in the book because it is frequented by many Ladywood people and contains one of the oldest remaining buildings in the area, Perrott's Folly. Many people who lived in this area regarded themselves as Ladywood people, although some regarded them as 'all kippers and curtains'!

So much for the extremities, but what about the heart of Ladywood? The bulk of the book includes scenes from the streets from what might be called central Ladywood, such as Monument Road, Ledsam Street, Great Tindal Street, Morville Street and St Vincent Street to name just a few. These streets contained the homes of the workers who made Birmingham the City of a Thousand Trades. There is no doubt that these streets have declined. Great Tindal Street, is hardly great, and Ledsam Street and St Vincent Street are but pale shadows of their former selves, thanks to the redevelopment of the 1960s.

Another wave of redevelopment in the last decade helped to put right some of the problems caused by the planners of the 1960s. This time the planners actively considered the views of local people. Today's community faces up to many problems and, as before the 1960s, residents have pulled together to help each other. Groups such as the Neighbourhood Forum, the Ladywood Social Club, St John's Church and the schools are thriving. One of our schools was recently singled out in Parliament as one of the best in the country.

I'm grateful to many of the present-day community for their help in compiling this book. I particularly acknowledge the support given to me by John Landon, George Elmer, Anthony Spettigue, Gordon Cull and Jim Cunningham: all of them and many more were in their 'oil-tot' when looking at the contributions.

Remember that this is a companion volume to *Britain in Old Photographs: Ladywood*, and many well-known buildings may be in volume one rather than here. This book fills a few gaps and expands on a few favourites. The response from the first book was so great that enough photographs already exist for a third! This is testimony to the former and current residents of Ladywood. Keep the photographs coming in via the publisher's address. I'm grateful to all who contributed, whether you regard yourself as from Ladywood . . . or Edgbaston, Spring Hill or Brookfields!

1

Street Scenes & People

Olive, David, Stephen and Alan Jones in the yard of 3 back of 34 St Mark's Street, *c.* 1952.

A Boys' Brigade march possibly in Ellen Street looking towards Spring Hill, *c.* 1949. (*Albert Mousdale*)

The Maple Leaf florist shop on the corner of George Street West and Spring Hill, 17 August 1967. Flowers were popular at that time. 'San Francisco', better known as 'Be Sure to Wear Flowers in Your Hair', was enjoying a four week run as Number One in the Hit Parade. St Peter's Church which was erected in 1901–2 stands behind the shop. The building on the right of the shop is the Coach & Horses pub.

Nos 55–62 Edward Street, August 1967. A.A. Howes' handyman's shop is on the corner of The Parade. The building with the pointed roof is the Lyric cinema. Adverts include one for Surf: 'down with prices, up with value' and Pintaman milk.

The bridge carrying the railway over Icknield Street at the junction with Pitsford Street as it looked in November 1974. One of the large adverts is for Ansells Bitter, which was advertised as being on sale in a 'man sized can'. Sadly it didn't explain how the thirsty men of the Midlands could open the can without the beer spurting all over the place! The bridge has since been replaced by another structure and carries the Metro en route from Snow Hill to Wolverhampton.

A mid-1960s street scene of George Street West taken from New Spring Street.

D. Ayre's on Ellen Street, August 1967. The writing above the doors states it was a 'groceries, provisions and general stores'. The windows are covered with typical adverts of the time, including Lyons Tea, Park Drive cigarettes and Midland Counties ice cream.

Spring Hill Passage, May 1964. The road sign indicates that a school was nearby; Steward Street School was just around the corner. The large advert sees kittens being used to advertise Cherry Blossom shoe polish.

The garage on the Sandpits between Clissold Street and Camden Street, 26 September 1955. This was the day that commercial television began in Britain and Gibbs toothpaste became famous as the first advert. Up until then posters were seen as the most effective form of advertising, with gable ends of buildings such as this one particularly popular sites.

Rosebery Street Tram Depot, March 1939. This depot could garage eighty-five trams and it opened in April 1906. Trams ran from it along Dudley Road, Hagley Road and on Ladywood's no. 33 route. The depot closed when the famous no. 33 route was taken over by buses in 1947. There is a photograph of the last tram on page 72 of *Ladywood in Old Photographs* (1999).

A no. 32 tram coming down Newhall Hill from the Jewellery Quarter, April 1939. It then turned on to Summer Row and trundled into the city centre. The King Edward VI pub which dates back to 1835 is on the left and Buckingham's factory is on the right. The Birmingham Corporation Social Club was once on Newhall Hill.

Mr Greaves, a man who has no doubt seen many changes, pauses for thought. This was taken in St Mark's Street in 1964. Former neighbour Marina Gilks recalls: 'He was always smartly dressed and he and his wife were so kind to my children.' (*Ingemar Lindahl*)

Alexandra Place in St Mark's Street, 7 June 1967. Earlier that week War Minister John Profumo resigned as a result of the Christine Keeler scandal. This no doubt gave these housewives something to talk about!

Islington Place on Anderton Street, 1937–8. Back row, left to right: Teddy Pyatt, Maud Checkley, Eileen Phillips, Gladys Checkley. Front row: Leslie Checkley, Dennis Checkley, Morris Parker. The little girl at the front is Doreen Yates. Leslie Checkley says 'As kids we made our own entertainment playing leap-frog, hopping Jimmy, door knocking, Polly on the mop stick and jackstones. Some of today's games were also popular such as yo-yos, marbles and I spy. Kick-the-can was always great fun. We kicked a can as far as we could and the rest ran off to hide and we had to get the can then go searching for our mates. We also played bowls using bicycle wheels. For 2d an hour you could hire a bike from a shop on the corner of Clement Street.'

Frankie McNally walking up St Mark's Street towards Shakespeare Road, 1955. There is an election poster on his far left – that's the far left of the wall and not necessarily the political standpoint of the person mentioned! It is not possible to read the candidate's name, but a General Election was held that year and Victor Yates, who had been MP for Ladywood since the Second World War, was re-elected. (*Billy Codling*)

Anderton Street, October 1964. This picture and others like it filled the pages of the local press as a prelude to a visit to the area by Housing Minister Richard Crossman. Front page stories about housing and redevelopment problems were rife. After the ministerial visit, which took in Anderton Street and Chamberlain Gardens, Victor Yates MP said: 'There is no doubt that the Minister was shocked at what he saw.' Twelve months earlier local people were being urged to set up resident associations to get their feelings across to the city council. Canon Norman Power was most active in supporting local people. A petition signed by four hundred women called for the immediate improvement of the neighbourhood around St Mark's Street. At this time a television play about inner city homelessness called *Cathy Come Home* was partly filmed in Hingeston Street. When it was broadcast in 1966 it caused a major furore and a Ladywood councillor protested to the BBC that Ladywood was chosen to represent Britain's slum conditions. The play led to a rethink in the way homeless people were treated by the authorities. (*John Landon*)

Nos 64–72 St Mark's Street in June 1967. This was the junction between 'Big' and 'Little' St Mark's Street at King Edward's Road. The Salvation Army often played beneath the street light. (*John Landon*)

Anderton Street, 1963. Josephine Codling is holding son Ricky and friend's son David Bannister on the right. This was outside their house at no. 115. (*Billy Codling*)

Hickman's the greengrocer on the corner of Nelson Street and King Edward's Road, just before the First World War. People on the left include George Rafferty, May Woodward, née Hickman and May Hickman. Sadly the most prominent man at the front is unidentifiable, but the man next to him with the cloth cap is Charlie Wheeler. He lived in Beach Street and worked there until the outbreak of the next world war.

Springfield Street, 6 May 1964. While Britain's seaside resorts cleared up after the Bank Holiday invasion of Mods and Rockers, the people from the back streets of Ladywood got on with their lives and the milkman and coalman continued their deliveries. The building on the right is The Crown pub on the corner of Cope Street. (*John Landon*)

In 1964 a group of Swedish students worked with Summerhill Methodist church to create a play area for local children. This is one of the photographs from their visit. It was taken in the Anderton Street/St Mark's Street area. (*Ingemar Lindahl*)

On Monument Road near the Station Inn not far from the corner of Cope Street. The clue to this location lies on the richly advertised walls. The Corn Stores are at 382 Monument Road, which is listed in the street directories as a bird and animal dealer. Next door is a pawnbroker and behind the bus there is a bootmaker and a baker.

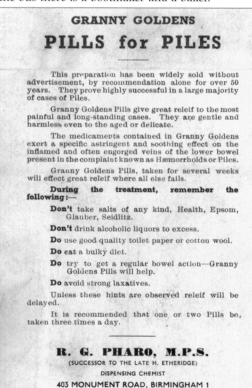

GRANNY GOLDENS
PILLS for PILES

This preparation has been widely sold without advertisement, by recommendation alone for over 50 years. They prove highly successful in a large majority of cases of Piles.

Granny Goldens Pills give great relief to the most painful and long-standing cases. They are gentle and harmless even to the aged or delicate.

The medicaments contained in Granny Goldens exert a specific astringent and soothing effect on the inflamed and often engorged veins of the lower bowel present in the complaint known as Hæmorrhoids or Piles.

Granny Goldens Pills, taken for several weeks will effect great relief where all else fails.

During the treatment, remember the following :—

Don't take salts of any kind, Health, Epsom, Glauber, Seidlitz.

Don't drink alcoholic liquors to excess.

Do use good quality toilet paper or cotton wool.

Do eat a bulky diet.

Do try to get a regular bowel action—Granny Goldens Pills will help.

Do avoid strong laxatives.

Unless these hints are observed relief will be delayed.

It is recommended that one or two Pills be taken three times a day.

R. G. PHARO, M.P.S.
(SUCCESSOR TO THE LATE H. ETHERIDGE)
DISPENSING CHEMIST
403 MONUMENT ROAD, BIRMINGHAM 1

Much to the relief of many local people Pharo the Chemist was located near to the junction of King Edward's Road and Monument Road. Granny Golden's last pills were popped in 1965 and the remaining piles were removed by the demolition men, that's piles of rubble of course!

This undated picture shows the Ledsam Street post office. It looks as though the last stamp had been licked and the shop was ready for demolition, so it was probably taken in about 1965. Ledsam Street runs off to the right and St Vincent Street to the left. Sherborne Street is on the far left. (*John Landon*)

The junction of St Vincent Street, Great Tindal Street and Browning Street, 1 April 1954. St Vincent Street runs off to the left over the canal bridge. The letters W.T.F. can just be seen on a factory sign. This was the Mysto Works of the implement makers W.T. French. (*John Landon*)

St Vincent Street from near the junction with Ledsam Street. Johnstone Street is in the distance and behind it demolition has taken place to reveal the buildings on Wood Street. This was taken from outside Dr Glass's surgery. Louis Glass became a councillor for Ladywood and was Lord Mayor from 1963 to 1964.

St Margaret's Church at the corner of Ledsam Street and Alston Street, seen from Great Tindal Street. Rann Street runs behind the church. The church was consecrated in 1875, the year Joseph Chamberlain started the Corporation Street development and Small Heath Alliance FC was formed, later to become Birmingham City. (*John Landon*)

Great Tindal Street, looking from Monument Road towards Mary Street on the right, November 1960.

An aerial view showing the junction of Ledsam Street and Great Tindal Street as it looks today. The junction is just to the left of the tower block. St Margaret's Church stood where the block now stands. The pathway down the middle of the photograph takes the route once occupied by Alston Street. Johnstone Street once cut across Alston Street and the pathway that runs across the lower part of the photograph marks the approximate line it once took.

At the junction of Johnstone Street and Rann Street, 19 January 1959. Rann Street, er, ran off to the right.

Nos 133–6 Ladywood Road at the corner with Rann Street, April 1974. The posters on the wall are election posters. In recent years Ladywood has had a number of well-known MPs; these have included Baroness Doris Fisher and former TV presenter Brian Walden. The current MP is Clare Short. Wallace Lawler was a distinguished local councillor who became MP for Ladywood at the by-election caused by the death of Victor Yates in 1969. In so doing he became the city's first Liberal MP since 1885. Ladywood was the smallest constituency in the country at the time, mainly because over 2,000 people had moved out of the area since the electoral register had been drawn up.

Lucy Grigg and members of the family outside their home in Morville Street, *c.* 1905. Baby Albert and his older brother both became draymen at Mitchell's and Butler's brewery. (*Gordon Cull*)

The scene from a backyard off Grosvenor Street West, September 1961.

A wedding celebration in Morville Street, late 1920s.

Sam Palmer was a road repair man and is seen here with push bike on Monument Road while undertaking pavement repair work in 1929. The bike was the only form of transport for the workers. Here workers' coats are being transported from one section to another. (*George Palmer*)

Monument Road was one of the great shopping streets of not just Ladywood, but of the whole of Birmingham. This is George Mason's as it looked in 1923. It was located near to the junction with Icknield Port Road. Beryl Gussinklo (née Bolten) says: 'My father is on the immediate right. He was a sixteen-year-old errand boy at the time and lived in Eldon Road.' The adverts tell of an 'important reduction in George Mason's Bacon'. This was no rash decision because it had to compete against Finest Danish Smoked Streaky!

A postcard showing the junction of Monument Road and Great Tindal Street at the Stour Valley pub, 1904. The pub proudly proclaims it was established in 1854. If you bought volume one of this series you will have read that the pub was generally known as The Horsefalls, popular belief being that a horse died outside it in 1947. This may well be true, but the landlord of the pub when this photograph was taken was J. Horsfall! Opposite stands a branch of Lloyds Bank on Beach Street corner.

Monument Road as it looked on a postcard used in 1909, but the view dates from about five years earlier as it is in the same series as the postcard on the previous page. The largest building on the left is the swimming baths which opened in 1883. On the opposite side of the road is the New Connexion Methodist Chapel. The advert on the extreme right is on the wall of a hay and straw dealer and is for 'Spratt's Patent Chicken Meal'. The shops on the left were a hosier, draper and a boot and shoemaker. The group of people look like priests on the way from the Oratory.

'My Old Man's A Dustman' was top of the hit parade on 21 April 1960 when this photograph was taken. For Bernard Ricketts it was definitely true! His 'old man', Bill Ricketts, really was a dustman and drove dustcart 247, which is the one pictured here on Monument Road. The Duke of Wellington pub is on the corner of Leach Street.

Summerhill Methodist Church on Monument Road, 1964. The line of buildings stretches as far as the Station Inn on the corner of Cope Street. The City of Birmingham Maternity & Welfare Centre, which is one of the buildings at a peculiar angle to the street, is the only building which is still standing today. (*Ingemar Lindhal*)

Inside Summerhill Methodist church hall, 1958. The 36th Boys' Brigade are taking part in a first aid class under the leadership of teacher Les Binnell. He was the first aid officer, bandmaster and photographer. Among the class are John Seal, David Dark, Michael Bates, Peter Hatch, Trevor 'Johnnie' Ray, David Wakeling, Paddy Quigley and Graham Bird. (*Albert Mousdale*)

Bill Landon & Sons bathroom shop is next to Holder's garage on Freeth Street, August 1967. Landon's pulled the plug on these premises and moved up the road into the former Crown cinema where there was extra space to expand and project a more upmarket image. Over eighty different bathroom and toilet suites can be viewed, but there is no lady with a torch to show you to your seat.

Lillian Carleton, Mary Fisher and Dolly Lovatt in Beach Street, *c.* 1960. Lindy Dunnett recalls: 'Dolly was the licensee of the outdoor at the bottom of Beach Street. As a youngster I used to help them to do the books and occasionally helped change the barrels and fill the jugs for them. We thought the building was upmarket because it had a bathroom!' (*Lindy Dunnett née Carleton*)

Oxford Terrace off Icknield Square, August 1967. John Landon recalls: 'The Blewitt family lived at the far end and my uncle Freddie, Freddie Handley, lived at the first house behind the car.' (*John Landon*)

A nicely framed view of 53–4 Freeth Street, 15 October 1965. There is very little play space for the little lad, but he may well have been about to recreate all of West Brom's goals following that week's impressive 4–1 victory over Sunderland. (*John Landon*)

George Thorp says: 'This is my dad, George Thorp Senior, on Beach Street looking towards Freeth Street on a Summer's evening in about 1949. He was on his way to the Duke, that's the Duke of Wellington pub where he used to be secretary of the darts team. A familiar sight then was a wife with old slippers and headscarf trudging wearily up this hill with a jug of ale covered with a tea towel!' The outdoor is at the bottom right corner. George Senior worked for fifty years as a candlestick maker. (*George Thorp*)

Part of the Beach Street gang, *c.* 1946. George Thorp says: 'There were gangs all over Ladywood, but they shouldn't be confused with teenage gang violence which erupted throughout Britain in the late '50s. These gangs were groups of lads who did things together like visiting the Ledsam or Crown picture houses, or they recaptured the jam factory from defending Germans and then wrestled crocodiles in the "rezza"! Our imagination was unlimited!' From left to right: Reggie Stephens, Harold Branson, Brian Stephens and Keith Bolton. (*George Thorp*)

Mrs May Hickman at Hickman's the greengrocer on Monument Road. When this shop was demolished the business was relocated to the new shopping parade on St Vincent Street opposite the new St John's School. The shop closed on Christmas Eve 2000, thus ending nearly a century of serving the local community. The first shop was set up at the Broad Street end of Sheepcote Street in about 1901. It moved to the premises pictured on page 16 in about 1909.

Ralph Hickman and staff at the Monument Road premises. At its peak there were two shops on Monument Road as well as the King Edward's Road shop.

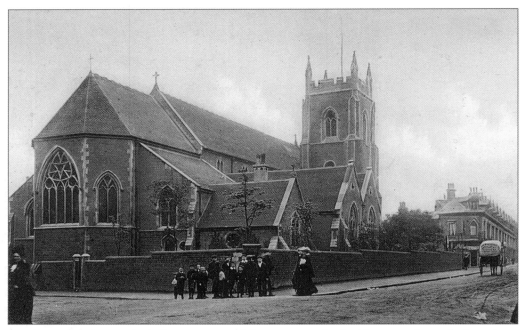

St John's Church as it looked on a postcard from 1904. The buildings on the right have been replaced by the offices of the Birmingham Hospital Saturday Fund. In 1904 they consisted of a tobacconist, tailor, bookmaker, dressmaker and a chemist. In case of emergencies there was also a plumber and a midwife, although both would presumably not be necessary for the same emergency!

A wedding at St John's Church, c. 1938. Left to right: Richard Cull, Hannah Cull, -?-, Bernard Cull, Alfred Cull, Teresa Harley, -?-, Ivy Cull, -?-, Alfred Harley.

The Revd Norman Darrell, who became vicar of St John's Church in 1940. He was succeeded by Canon Norman Power in 1952. He is pictured with his wife and two sons at the church in June 1951. The church history records him presiding over 'the tragic war years, the evacuation, the great shift of population which followed, the disruption of life and the many evil influences of the war which had a terrible effect on the district'.

Wood Street from Monument Road in January 1961. St John's Church is on the right.

The chapel at St Philip's Orphanage on Oliver Road. This is one of four postcards depicting scenes from the orphanage. (*Mary Crossley*)

The boys' lavatory at St Philip's Orphanage. This is possibly the most unusual Ladywood scene ever to be turned into a postcard! (*Mary Crossley*)

A group at St Philip's Orphanage. I expect you may have noticed the rather large white hats, or wimples, which the nuns are wearing! (*Mary Crossley*)

The boys' reading room at the Orphanage. (*Mary Crossley*)

Noel Road on a postcard which dates from about 1905. The waterworks tower is in the distance.

A group of happy children playing in Hyde Road. People will always say how safe it was to play on the streets, but times were changing. This was taken in October 1965, the same month that the infamous Moors Murderers appeared in court.

Coxwell Road, 1947–8. George Palmer says: 'This is my father, Sam. He was a chauffeur for four years. The car is a Packard belonging to Joe Whitall, a builder from Lancaster Street.' (*George Palmer*)

A postcard view of Coxwell Road. This road ran between Reservoir Road and Hyde Road. Oliver Road ran off it and led to the Orphanage and Grammar School. Today the street has been realigned and named Coxwell Gardens.

Osler Street, August 1961. This end of terrace building was a beer retailer, more commonly known as the 'outdoor'. At this time the name above the door read 'Mrs Rose Olds'. The terrace of houses on the right is Reservoir Avenue.

Looking up Osler Street from the Icknield Port Road Junction, March 1968. The café would have been popular with workers from Winfield's which was opposite it. Faded lettering on one of the buildings can be deciphered as 'Lilley & Stenson' garage. This was taken in the week that the government introduced legislation to fight increasing crime and burglary and first introduced the slogan 'Watch Out, There's A Thief About'. (*John Landon*)

Flossie and Ivy Cull with bird cage at Heathcliff Place on Osler Street, April 1930. Ivy became a bus conductress in the Second World War and later took a single ticket to New Zealand.

Rose Cull's wedding to Thomas Thorpe in Osler Street. Nan and Grandad are on the extreme right of the back row. (*Gordon Cull*)

Coplow Street, 1918. This photograph features three families from the street, the Wards, the Bartletts and the Goldings. The soldier is Bill Bartlett, brother of the sisters on the front row. It was possibly taken during a visit home from the First World War trenches. (*Len Ward*)

Nos 17–27 Coplow Street during demolition. This was taken in August 1971. (*Birmingham City Council collection*)

A no. 33 tram on Icknield Port Road near to the Dudley Road junction. The last tram on this route ran in August 1947 and was replaced by the no. 95 bus. Cath Brennan recalls: 'We used to sometimes be woken up at 4.00 a.m. by the sound of the first tram. This was a special tram which used to water the tracks. I think it was used to keep the dust down and may have helped the friction on the wheels, but I'm not sure. I do know they always came at the same time in the morning. We used to say you could put your clock on it.'

Icknield Port Road near Coplow Street, 1961. The Fordson van advertises Kennomeat, while the shops advertise the typical products of the day, including Echo margarine. By contrast, notice the drab frontage of Dalton's 'turf commissioners' – 'the bookies' were no go areas for many! The gap between the buildings leads to Railway Terrace, where children may well have been listening to *Children's Hour* which was dropped by the BBC on this day – 8 February 1961 – after nearly forty years.

Dominant features of this scene are the railway and canal to the left and Icknield Port Road, which runs down from the right and across to Dudley Road. At the junction of these two roads there is open space where Flint Tower, a residential block, was about to be built. The top of the picture is the industrial area around Rotton Park Street, and the dense terraced houses for the workers lie off Coplow and Marroway Streets. Part of Summerfield Park can be seen in the bottom right-hand corner.

A view of the rear of the terraces on Icknield Port Road between Monument Road and Freeth Street as they looked in 1965.

Ladywood police station on Ladywood Road, *c.* 1950. The posters advertise evening classes and call on the people to 'Join the Modern Army'.

A no. 33 tram on Ladywood Road. The road off to the left is St Vincent Street. Anthony Spettigue recalls: 'My grandmother used to get her pension from the post office, where the pillar box is located. She would rustle the crispy ten shilling note when she got back home!'

On Hagley Road with the now demolished Church of the Redeemer in the background. An advert on the tram is for 'Perfection Whisky', so perhaps you could have a wee dram on the tram if stuck in a jam?

Traffic congestion at the Ivy Bush. This was the scene in 1926 when a traffic island was introduced to help alleviate the growing problem. The island has since been removed, proving that some ideas just go round in circles.

Duchess Road on an undated postcard.

A sedate trot along the Hagley Road near the Oratory captured on a postcard which was postmarked July 1905. Horse-drawn buses were gradually phased out after the introduction of motor buses in 1903.

A view of the Oratory which was printed as a paper Christmas card in 1964 and used again in later years. It bears the message 'with every good wish from Father Phillip Lynch'. (*Mary Crossley*)

The Oratory choir, 1936. Back row: this includes Messrs Ward, Bujac and Hewitt. Third row, left to right: Bernard Bornorino, Arthur Davenport, Frank Lewis, George Ardagh, Alberto Bonorino, Frank Hayward, Mr Manighetti, Denis Saunders, Albert Reynolds, John Ramsell. Second row: George Jones, Charles Burns, Bernard Bradley, H.B. Collins, Rev. Fr Robert Eaton, Joe Green, Clem Dillon, Mr Wyre, Fred Green. The lad at the end of the front row is called Brady. Philip Crossley, who supplied the postcard, was a member of the choir for nearly sixty years.

A new motor bus on Hagley Road just past the Ivy Bush pub. This is from a postcard of about 1905. All the buildings are still standing today, although the road is now a major dual carriageway. Anthony Spettigue says: 'In the late 1950s these shops were frequented by the rich in their Rolls-Royces!'

This postcard shows a conductor and driver proudly posing for a view of a 'new motor bus' which ran along Hagley Road. It was addressed to an aunt in Rugby by Esther. She wrote: 'sending you the photo of one of our buses. We shall be very pleased to see any of you this holiday. Then we can take you for a ride, they are very nice.'

Five Ways on a postcard dated 1906. The statue is of Joseph Sturge (1793–1859), a well known anti-slave campaigner and creator of an adult school at Severn Street. It was estimated that over 10,000 people turned up to see the statue unveiled in June 1862. The other figures represent Peace and Charity. The statue was moved to another nearby location in front of what is now the Marriott Hotel when the Five Ways underpass was built. Not so lucky were the buildings on the right, all destroyed in the name of progress. One of those buildings was King Edward's School, which dates back to 1883.

Five Ways, 1923. Only the clock survived the 1970s redevelopment, although its position has moved slightly. The shops on the left have been demolished. Sawers the fishmonger was, in later years, the best-known shop on this row. (*Albert Trap*)

2

Ladywood Schools

Break time detention at Oratory School, 1959.

St Mark's Street School, 1933. The children include Winnie Colley and Ron Saunders, who are on the left of the back row and Kenny Waldron, the blond lad in the centre of the middle row, while those on the front row include Ken Bates, the twins Kenny and Stanley James and Nora Norton. The school closed in 1940. (*Ron Saunders*)

Brookfield's Junior and Infants School in Ellen Street at the time of the official opening in October 1950. It replaced the Victorian building which was destroyed in 1940. The Minister of Education, George Tomlinson MP, opened the new 'Brookies' in the same week that the House of Commons was reopened by the king after it too had suffered war damage. In October 1950 it was announced that teachers' salaries would be increased to £630 for men and £504 for women! Class sizes at the time were considerably larger than the one shown in the photo, which was obviously taken for publicity purposes.

Oratory School Infant department teachers in the hall of the building on Hyde Road, 1920. Mrs Reynolds is the teacher who is standing up. Two of the other three are Miss Bailey on the left and Miss Mayes in the middle. In those days female teachers were usually forced to give up the job when they married. It is suggested that Mrs Reynolds was able to continue teaching because she may have been a war widow, but we cannot be sure. (*Mary Crossley*)

The Oratory School shortly before demolition. The school dates back to about 1856, but this part of the building is the section built in 1947 when it was enlarged and divided into secondary modern, junior and infants departments. The infants entered through the door on the left.

A class in part of the old St John's Junior School, November 1963. The new school opened in 1961 and was originally called Ladywood County Primary School; however, it soon reverted to the name it was given when it first opened in 1857, St John's. (*John Landon*)

Green-fingered pupils at the new St John's School greenhouse, July 1970. The headteacher on the right is Miss Smethurst. (*Birmingham City Council collection*)

Nelson Street School, 1947. Three members of the class are Georgie Bevan, David Swingler and Margaret Owen. (*Keith Barr*)

Nelson School, February 1967. This building was erected as Nelson Street Board School in 1876 and was altered on numerous occasions. In 1894 a newspaper report stated: 'In Birmingham you may recognise a Board school by its being the best building in the neighbourhood. With lofty towers which serve the utilitarian purpose of giving excellent ventilation, gabled windows, warm red bricks and stained glass the best of Birmingham's Board schools have quite an artistic finish.' (*John Landon*)

Nelson Primary School, January 1974. The artistic merit of the original building seems to have disappeared, although the playground is enhanced by a dead tree. The picture below was taken from the roof of the tower block in this picture. The block is Durham Tower, where the Pink Panther is rumoured to be a resident . . . Durham, Durham, Durham, Durham, Durham. . . .

Nelson Primary School as it looks today. Budding athletes need only look across the road to be inspired, as the school is in the shadow of the National Indoor Arena. It was opened in October 1991 by sprinter Linford Christie. Sprinters on the track run over Sprinters of a different kind, because Sprinter trains make tracks on the main Birmingham to Wolverhampton railway which runs beneath the arena. The ugly buildings either side of it are the car parks, prompting one local wag to suggest that NIA stands for Naff Insensitive Architecture!

The George Dixon schools on City Road on a postcard stamped January 1918. The school moved to this site in 1906 after vacating premises on Oozells Street. The Oozells Street building recently became the new Ikon Gallery, part of the Brindleyplace development. Many people complain of waiting a long time to catch a no. 11 bus on City Road. The people in this picture would certainly be in for a long wait because the service didn't start running until eight years after this picture was taken!

There is no bus in this photograph either, but there is a conductor. He is conducting the George Dixon School orchestra in 1954. The school magazine for July 1954 states: 'a wide variety of demands upon the theatre section – each necessitated a fresh repertoire, and often at extremely short notice – tested to the full the ability and keenness of the senior members. There was an excellent response and special praise is merited by the leaders of each section.'

A netball team at St Peter's School, *c.* 1945. Kathy Ward, Doreen Murphy, Doreen Gregory and Marion Keane are the girls on the back row. Cecilia Jones is in the middle of the front row. Next to her on the right is Nora Wilson. In later life Nora married at the adjacent St Peter's Church, and later gave birth to a lovely little lad who grew up to compile this book! (*Nora Bartlam*)

A class at St Peter's School, 1938. Pupils on the front row include C. Dalton, Agatha Pittaway, Gladys Tovey, Joan Kennedy, Winnie Daley, Christine Ryan, Joyce Andrews and Joan Richards. The second row features A. Millington, Florence Tovey and Olive O'Lauchlin. Pupils on the back row include ? Dalton, Harry Palmer, ? Gilbert, ? Higgins, M. O'Rourke, the Welch twins, H. Fowler, B. Mason. (*Joan Taylor née Kennedy*)

An undated photograph of Infants Group VIII at Barford Road Infants School. The school opened in 1887 and is still going strong today, although today there are considerably fewer than the 1,180 pupils which the building was designed to hold.

A violin class at Barford Road School, 1930. Len Ward recalls: 'The boy is my brother Walter and the girls either side of him are both called Elsie, Elsie Golding to the right and Elsie Fry on the left.' (*Len Ward*)

Barford Road School's team which competed against Selly Park Girl's School in a road safety competition in Summerfield Park in about 1954. (*Keith Barr*)

In the science laboratory at Barford Road School. 'Stephens Ink for All Temperatures' is written on the thermometer behind them. (*Keith Barr*)

Barford Road School, 1961. Back row, left to right: -?-, Alan Jones, Howard Winston, ? Wilkinson, Raymond Rassell, ? Thompson, Tony Moss, Mr Hepburn. Middle row: -?-, -?-, -?-, -?-, ? Robinson, Derek Helt, ? Harrison, John Bushell. Front row: Kelvin Cox, -?-, -?-, ? Gibbs, Freddie Yardley, ? Smith, -?-, -?-, -?-. (*Alan Jones*)

Steward Street School May Festival, 1933. Eva Iles, then Eva Dyson, says: 'I was about six when this was taken. I'm the girl on the front row at the right with a bow in my hair. I think this was a performance of either Little Bo Peep or Little Red Riding Hood which was a supporting play at the May Festival. Some of the other girls were my friends Doris Clemson, Ida Lacey and Irene Hancock. The girl behind me with the necklace on is Evelyn Startin.' (*Eva Iles*)

Christmas at Steward Street School, 1954. Standing, left to right: -?-, Tommy Wagstaffe, Alan Jones, Dolcie Dugmore, -?-, David Smith, Robert Birkett, -?-. Seated: Pat Carter, Danny Podmore, -?-. Lynn Evans is holding baby Jesus. Alan Jones recalls: 'I was six at the time and I had to walk in pointing at the star. This was performed in front of all the parents.' (*Alan Jones*)

The Steward Street School building as it looked in 1983. The building dates from 1873 and was big enough to hold 1,036 pupils. It closed as a school in about 1970. For a time the school turned to the arts as the basis of education, believing that the development of personality demanded greater attention then the 3Rs. (*Birmingham City Council collection*)

Osler Street School as it looked in about 1971. When the school opened in 1875 the packed timetable for Class One read as follows: 9.30 writing, 10.15 register, 10.30 arithmetic, 11.15 recreation, drill or singing, 11.30 reading, 12.00 geography, or grammar, 12.30 lunch, 2.00 tables, 2.30 writing, 3.00 arithmetic, 3.30 reading, 4.00 grammar or geography, 4.30 home lessons.

Osler Street School in March 1968, looking down towards Icknield Port Road. The school was named after Abraham Follett Osler, a worthy local citizen who had a glass manufactory in Freeth Street and an enormous showroom on Broad Street next to Lee Longland's present premises. He was also instrumental in setting up the instruments for the weather observatory at The Folly on Waterworks Road.

Girls at Osler Street School, 1920. An inspector's report, written in 1913, states: 'In spite of the fact that the girl are drawn from homes which make considerable demands on their energies outside of school hours, generally satisfactory work is being done.'

Boys at Osler Street School, 1921.

Osler Street School, *c.* 1921. Ivy Hunt is the six-year-old girl who is nearest to the camera. She left school at the age of fourteen and worked at Townson and Coxson in Essington Street making gas fittings until she got married and moved to Jersey. She is now eighty-five years old. Notice the dividing curtain which separates two classes. The blackboards on the rear wall have key spellings on them. The words on one board read street, house, shop, tram, horse and policeman. The other board includes the words morning, night, afternoon, evening, early and late. (*Albert Hunt*)

Osler Street School 1935. Beryl Gussinklo remembers: 'I was about six when this was taken. I'm the girl standing in front of the boy on the back row who has the large tie! I can remember some of the names: David McCormach, George Gibbons, Barbara Baldwin, Elsie King, Daphne Bedford, Betty Davenport, Irene Whittaker, Margaret Showell, Betty Bowen, Joan Hunt, Dorothy Dunne, Elsie Carr, Ann Wallbridge, Alfred Taylor and George Woodall.' (*Beryl Gussinklo, née Bolten*)

Osler Street Boys' School. Frank Hunt, who supplied the photograph, is in the middle of the second row from the front. He says: 'This was my class with our teacher Mr Thorne. I think I was about ten or eleven years old at the time and as I left school in 1940 at the age of fourteen it must mean that it was taken in 1936 or 1937.' (*Frank Hunt*)

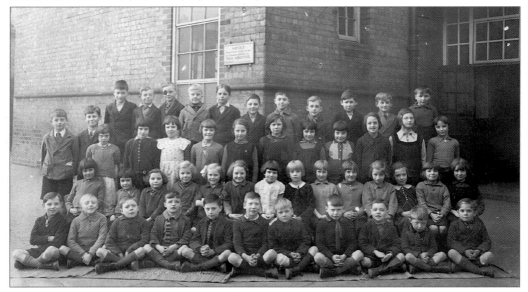

Osler Street Boys' School in the mid-1930s. The little lad second right on the front row is Derek Fowler. His brother Len is two along from him. Others include Freddie and Joan Hotchkins, Stanley and Ronnie Hunt, Rita Bodfish and Sylvia and Rachel Rodgers. Frank Hunt is also in this photograph: he is the one wearing the eye patch on the back row. The former pupil said: 'I had what they called a lazy eye and the patch was supposed to strengthen it. It didn't work and I often took some stick from my classmates for having to wear it.' (*Derek Fowler*)

How many of you remember receiving a school portrait photograph which came in one of these Christmas folders? Over the years many folders were lost, but photos remain. This one is of Osler Street pupil Barry Cull and dates back to 1946 or 1947. (*Gordon Cull*)

Osler Street School in about 1948. Allen Hewings recalls: 'I am one of those who has his hands on his mate's shoulders behind the teacher who was Mr Moss. Mr Marshall who was our headteacher is standing on the extreme right of this photo. We were about thirteen when this was taken.' (*Allen Hewings*)

Osler Street football team, 1947/8. Len Bryan, who is second left on the back row, remembers: 'It was a really good side at that time and we were photographed because we won the Birmingham Schools Cup. That is the big cup you can see on the picture. We beat Bierton Road School in the Final.' Back row, left to right: Gordon Hunt, Len Bryan, John Hyde, Ronnie Aston, Harold Ford and Dennis Pettitt. Front row: Roy White, Gerald Rogers, Eddie Harris, Freddie Woods, Johnnie Vale. (*Len Bryan*)

Osler Street junior football team, 1952/3. Back row, left to right: Hughes, King, Hedges, Wolsey, Jackson, -?-. Front row: Lee, Cull, -?-, -?-, Smith.

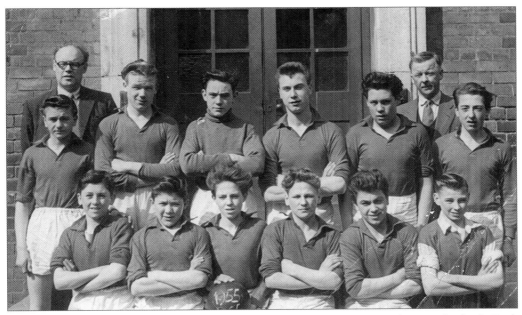

Osler Street Senior Boys, 1955/6. Mr Phipps and Mr Brenton are the teachers at the back. Back row, left to right: -?-, Brian Kelly, Barry Downes, Pete Close, Sam Bartram, Graham Cull. Front row: -?-, Robin Lane, Kenny Orme, John Weaver, Billy Codling, Joey Forrest.

Long-serving teacher Cecil Jones at Osler Street School, 1974. Pupils were preparing a mural in the run up to the school's centenary. It shows a phoenix rising from the ashes on a wall in the assembly hall. The building should have closed in 1972, but stayed open until 1978. It was first earmarked for demolition in 1948!

If anyone could make a meal of things it was these ladies, the dinner ladies at Osler Street School in the early 1960s. Chocolate concrete, semolina, boiled cabbage: can't you just smell it! The head cook, Mrs Whittington, is second left on the front row.

Lucy Cull, on the left, worked as a dinner lady at the school for about twenty years. The other lady is Marion Smith.

Teacher Paul Nagle in fashionable flared trousers and wide tie stands on the left of this group of Ladywood School pupils on a residential field trip to Bell Heath in 1977. Teachers will always tell you to watch the pupils on the back row: one in particular appears to need watching on this occasion!

Cricket-loving pupils from Ladywood School visited Worcester with teacher Mr Cross, and came across a man who could play a bit of cricket. His name? Viv Richards!

A staff group at Ladywood School. Headteacher Mr Welch is flanked by deputy headteachers Marjorie Heywood and Roger Perks.

Ladywood School developed a budding badminton star in Kevin Rowe. He received sponsorship from local paint company PPG, formerly Docker Brothers.

Ladywood School pupils Mark Bagnall, left and Dean Dodd met football manager Graham Taylor, then at Aston Villa, in April 1988 before the Football League centenary game, which was played at Villa Park between Villa and Birmingham City. Mr Taylor was interviewed by Villa-loving pupils for the school's newspaper *The Ladywood Bugle*. Aston Villa showed a sense of history on that occasion. It is a shame they didn't think of their history when they demolished the Witton Road stand.

The new intake at Ladywood School show off their uniforms to their parents, 1987. Left to right: Sandra Kiely, Debra Lines, Hayley Jones and three first-year boys.

Ladywood School's Patrick Flanagan, David Walker and Gary Knight hold the Birmingham School's Cup Shield in February 1987. Ladywood was by that time one of the smallest secondary schools in the city and in the final they played against one of the largest, Sheldon Heath. The result was a draw and both schools shared the trophy. The most exciting game was the quarter final when Ladywood went 2–0 down after eight minutes, but fought back to win 3–2 in extra time against Cockshutt Hill School.

The class of c. 1988. One of the classes at Ladywood School. Back row, left to right: Daljit Singh, Darran Burgwin, Mohammed Habib, form teacher and author of this book Norman Bartlam, Adam Beckford, -?-, Peter Jones, Lee Moult. Front row: -?-, -?-, -?-, -?-, Debbie ?, Kamaljit Kaur, Michelle Keeling, Helen Perkins and Cathy ? are seated on the wall around the fish pond.

It's the Ladywood Bugler, with pupil Scott McGough and the aforementioned *Ladywood Bugle*. This was taken as part of an army recruitment drive. The tallest tower belongs to the now demolished swimming baths, and the tower behind Scott is the practice tower at Ladywood Fire Station. The area of grass was left vacant for a primary school and ambulance station, but neither were built.

Cleaners at Ladywood School in 1990 celebrate fifty years' service between them. Left to right: Denise Bancroft, Silvanie Blackwood and Jean Turbill. Ten years on and Jean is still a cleaner in the building which is now Ladywood Arts and Leisure Centre.

Former Ladywood School pupil Maureen Pinto receives an employee of the month award from Barry Clevedon at the International Convention Centre.

Ladywood School News cameraman Mark Bartlett with reporter Daniel Millward on Broad Street on the day the bridge link was erected between the Hyatt Regency Hotel and the International Convention Centre. 'It's 7 February 1989 and the bridge has at last been lifted into position.'

3

Ladywood at Work

An aerial view of the industrial area off Icknield Port Road. Dominant factories include PPG Paints and Belliss & Morcom.

The railway yards looking towards Sheepcote Street, 7 October 1962. Part of the stables building can be seen at the top of the embankment on the left. (*Roger Carpenter*)

The railway sheds, again looking towards Sheepcote Street, but this time a few years earlier: this photograph was taken in about 1951. It is impossible to take a photograph from the same viewpoint today because one of the car parks for the National Indoor Arena has been built on this site. (*Roger Carpenter*)

D.T. Powell's sawmill at the railway siding near the junction of Monument Road and Cope Street, adjacent to the railway station, 1930s. (*Roger Carpenter*)

D.T. Powell's timber yard is in the background of this scene from 1951.

Canals played an important part in the industrial development of Ladywood before going into decline. Today they are a major tourist attraction and the area around Broad Street has won a number of awards. This location at Cambrian Wharf is now popular with tourists. The small building in the centre is the former tollhouse at the head of the Farmer's Bridge locks. The name refers not to the days when this was farming land but to the landowner, who was called Mr Farmer! The dominant building is the former glass works in Scotland Street called Parker and Osborn, which was converted into offices for Bucknall Austin.

Workers of B. Whitehouse & Sons, decorators and builders. Jim Taylor recalls: 'I'm fourth from the left at the back by the ladder on this photograph, which was taken at the AA building on Hagley Road in about 1951. After we had finished that job we worked on the renovation of Docker Brothers' factory, which had been badly damaged in the war. B. Whitehouse & Sons was based in Waterworks Road.' (*Jim Taylor*)

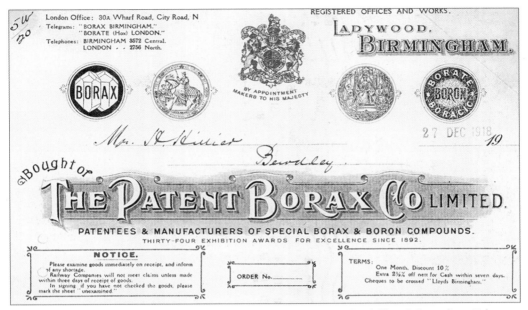

The Patent Borax Company was located on Ledsam Street, and this billhead dates from February 1919.

Burton & Cole motor dealers on Ruston Street, January 1975. The factory has been replaced by housing. Other occupants of the street such as the A1 Screw Company, Munslow & Holder scrap iron merchants and Andrew & Hopkins toolmakers have also been demolished. The only recognisable feature on the photograph which remains to this day is the white corner post which stands at the corner of Rawlins Street outside The Vine pub. (*Birmingham City Council collection*)

The first lorry to be purchased by George Sykes's timber merchants in Sheepcote Street in about 1915. It was a 36–40 hp 5 ton Leyland truck. 'It ran for twenty three and a half years without mechanical failure.' (*Sykes Timber*)

Sykes's more modern lorry at the Sheepcote Street works, 1953. (*Sykes Timber*)

Birmingham was often called the 'City of a Thousand Trades' and most of those trades probably went on in the streets of Ladywood, where the working man manufactured many innovative and time-saving machines. This lawnmower was said to be a cut above the rest and was manufactured in Sheepcote Street at Ewell's, which advertised itself as 'The City Iron, Hurdle & Fencing works'.

Sheepcote Street as it looked at the end of the twentieth century. The now derelict Hudson Edmunds Tube works dominated this part of the street. The row of buildings is being held up by scaffolding, not because they are listing, but because of their architectural listing. The Albion pub and Foxall's café were the former occupants.

Sheepcote Street, April 1958. Baxter's bolts, screws and rivets works dominates this scene. Baxter's closed in about 1969. A van belonging to Pearce & Cutler is parked opposite one of their buildings. The bus stop was used by the no. 19 city circle route which crossed Broad Street and went down Granville Street. George Elmer remembers: 'Sheepcote Street was popular with us when we were kids because it was one of the few streets in the district which was always tarmaced. This was important to us because it didn't have a cobbled surface so it was great for us roller skaters!'

Pearce & Cutler glass dates back to 1815, through the Pearce family business. Solomon and Ephram Cutler built up a separate business and the two firms amalgamated in 1920. The large glass sections were manhandled using special leather carrying straps. (*Clive Cutler*)

Workers are jammed in at the Canning & Wildblood jam factory in Freeth Street. In this scene mainly women workers are canning the fruit. The factory was popular with local children. One of them was George Thorp who lived in Beach Street. He explains: 'It was the tins which were popular with us youngsters! As the horse and carts came down the street we used to distract the men and nick the cans as well as the fruit. The cans were very useful to put the tiddlers in when we went to the reservoir!' (*John Landon*)

Bowkett's bread van, 1936. Bowkett's was located on Broad Street, near St Martins Street, from at least the 1870s until it was bombed out in the Second World War. George Binnion is with the horse-drawn van which took him on deliveries around the streets of Ladywood and Edgbaston. He was caretaker at the bakery and lived over the shop. A stables for five horses led out on to Tennant Street. (*Alan Binnion*)

D.H. Hall moved into the former Holmes printing premises after being bombed out in the Second World War. They improved the premises and expanded their business. The firm was passed down by at least nine generations of the Hall family and was once the seventh oldest company still trading in the city, dating back to at least 1767.

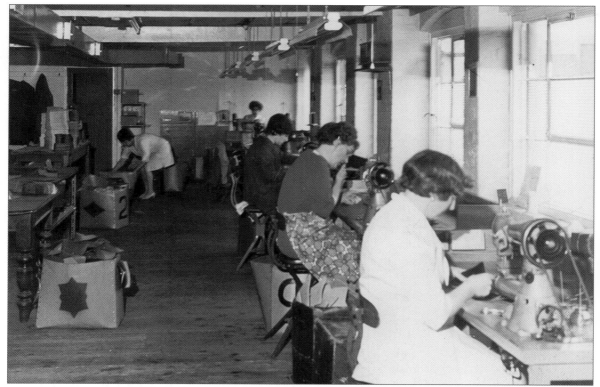

Workers manufacturing spectacle cases at the D.H. Hall premises in Freeth Street. Evelyn Clifford is at the front and Margaret Dyke, Mary O'Connor and Sheila Davies sit alongside her.

The Montil Manufacturing Company was established in Morville Street just before the outbreak of the First World War. They prided themselves on their 'perfect British toys'. A 1930 advertising brochure stated that the Gee-Gee Kar, on the right, was 'a very popular toy for the lovers of horses' and was 'beautifully furnished in white washable cellulose'. The Push Motor Car was 'a handsome motor car of ever increasing popularity for children aged 4–6 years'.

Stern & Bell engravers in Stour Street, March 1961. Also on the street at that time were well-known firms such as Belldar engineering, J.W. Howard woodworkings and Rooke metalspinners.

Belliss & Morcom originated on Broad Street and, just like the steam from their engines, expanded. The expansion into Ledsam Street was successful and they eventually moved into Icknield Square. The Ledsam Street building still bears their name in the brickwork on the front of the building. This advertisement dates from 1878.

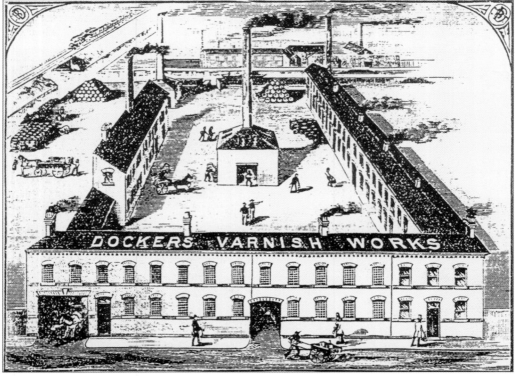

Docker Brothers paint factory as it looked in an industrial magazine in 1888. The text stated: 'Ample staffs of skilled work people are constantly engaged and varnishes, paints and lacquers are being sent to all parts of the country. The members of the firm are well-known locally in social and commercial circles, and are in receipt of that respect and esteem which is the just reward of ability, energy, and enterprise.'

The Mint on Icknield Street as it looked on a postcard dated December 1915. The text on the back reads: 'I suppose you've heard by now that I have started at this place shown on the other side. I am assistant analytical chemist. It isn't half an easy job. This is not all of our works, only about half of them, as a lot more mills etc. are on the other side of the road.'

Wildman & Meguyer Ltd were located on the Sandpits near to Camden Street. All types of enamel signs were manufactured. This advertisement dates from 1909.

Barrett's Old Fashioned Brewed Ginger Beer came from the Barrett's Country Bottling Co. Ltd, which was located on St Vincent Street near to the junction with Johnstone Street. It was there from at least 1886 until the early 1930s. A stores was located on Rann Street. I found this bottle on display in a pub in Ireland. The pub is now minus one artefact, but there are more of them on display at Danny Byrne's pub in Mullingar.

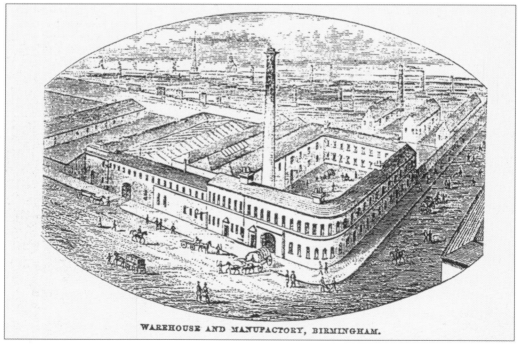

WAREHOUSE AND MANUFACTORY, BIRMINGHAM.

Baldwin's Paper Bag manufactory in Morville Street as it looked on a letterhead dated 1888. At that time James Baldwin advertised his patent Square-Bottomed Paper Bags, which were said to 'stand unrivalled as the best article in the trade'.

All we know about this is that it was taken in about 1930 and Gordon Cull, who supplied the photograph, knows that his grandad is third from the left on the second row and his father is standing in the middle of the row behind him. Grandad was a master builder and his father a builder. It was possibly taken during the construction of the flats opposite the Ivy Bush which are known as Kenilworth Court.

This is a total mystery. It comes from the Cull family of Osler Street. Which company would have a large stores like this? Can anyone help identify it?

A foundry in Steward Street, November 1966. The man on the left is Denis Black. (*John Landon*)

Oozells Street North as it looked as the building faced demolition in 1986. The main occupiers of these premises were Hunt & Mitton, the valve manufacturers. The large factory at the end of the street with the chimney was the Atlas Works. Back-to-back houses once stood on the opposite side of the road. These were demolished by the time this photograph was taken. The area had become a car park used by visitors to Bush House, the Housing Department headquarters based on Broad Street. Today the whole area lies under the BT offices at Brindleyplace.

4

Ladywood Leisure

Preparing for bonfire night in Summerfield Park, October 1970.

The main lending section on the ground floor of Spring Hill Library in June 1968. The library first opened in January 1893. (*Birmingham City Council collection*)

The interior of the reading room in the upstairs of Spring Hill Library, 13 June 1968. A week earlier the newspapers were full of the story of the shooting of Senator Robert Kennedy, brother of JFK, while the hunt for the killer of Martin Luther King ended with the arrest of James Earl Ray. The sports pages featured Allan Clarke who became England's most expensive player after moving from Fulham to Leicester for £150,000.

The entrance to Edgbaston Reservoir as it looked on a postcard dated October 1904. A 1920 publication noted: 'in connection with the grounds there is a very fine skating rink and entertainment hall'. Around the time the photograph was taken the Birmingham Skating Club held winter skating events on the ice. In 1902 the press reported: 'to the delight of those who have the time, the health and the leisure to go a-skating the frost continues'. Robert Hall was said to be 'the prince of local skaters'. He was educated at the proprietary school on Hagley Road and taught early morning writing classes at Nelson Street School.

The bandstand at Edgbaston Reservoir on a postcard dated 1905.

Happy days at the 'rezza', *c.* 1952. Back row, left to right: Freddie Griffin, John Farrington, Frankie Bolton, Harry Smith, Danny Gilmore, Alan Welsh. Front row: Freddie Gibbs, -?-, Freddie Wilkes. (*John Landon*)

John Beale, in the centre wearing a white shirt, steers his boat at the Regatta Day at the Reservoir, 1958. (*Janet Beale née Taylor*)

John and Carl Elliott outside Carl's house in Daisy Road, preparing to head off for the Sea Cadets at TS *Vernon*, based at Edgbaston Reservoir. (*Janet Beale née Taylor*)

At the Tower Ballroom, 1972. Left to right: B. Perry, T. Cunningham, J. Cunningham, S. Cunningham, G. Quirke, T. Sullivan, N. Howells, R. McCullough. Number one hits that summer included 'Puppy Love' by Donny Osmond and 'Mama Weer All Crazee Now' from Slade, while Jim Cunningham, the caretaker at the Oratory School, would have enjoyed singing the current hit, Alice Cooper's 'School's Out for Summer'. (*Sadie Cunningham*)

An early 1950s snap of the staff at the Tower Ballroom. The lady third from the right is Ivy Kennedy, the manageress of the bar. Mr Thompson and Mr Dutton stand next to her. One of the other staff is Gladys Bird; she is second from the left. (*Gordon Cull*)

Staff from the canteen of Wiggins' in Wiggin Street enjoy a night out at the Tower Ballroom with friends and partners in about 1956. Second from the right is Frank Bartlam, soon to be married to Nora Wilson who is behind him. They later became the parents of the author of this book. (*Nora Bartlam*)

A postcard produced by the ice rink on Summerhill. Keen skater Bill Cokayne recalls: 'Gary Owen was one of about six professional skaters at the time and he can clearly be seen holding a girl's hand to show her how to keep her stance. This photograph was taken from the big balcony looking towards the entrance. There was a big café on the right with glass windows which enabled you to see what was going on while you were eating their lovely egg and chips!'

A crowd at the ice rink, early 1960s. The Ladywood people include, from left to right, Barry Butler, Ron Kelly, Tommy Lundy, Bill Parry, Brian Lambert, Frank Lundy with glass, Kenny Banner, Bobby Arkel. The skating rink closed in 1964. The local press said: 'One of the main attractions of the City's entertainment world is closing its doors today after thirty-four years.' Mecca, the owners, were quoted as blaming 'the dying area of Ladywood' for the closure. (*Ron Kelly*)

The Northern Ice Dance team, which became runners-up in the league in 1959. Team members included Arthur Jeffries, Peggy Hitchins, Dena Hargreaves, Don Baker, Roy Mason and Mary Parry. (*Peggy Hitchins*)

Celebrating the twenty-first anniversary of the Birmingham Ice Dance Club. (*Peggy Hitchins*)

Ladywood Swimming Baths on Monument Road, July 1979. The datestone above the door reads 1940.

Tony the Tiger and Olympic swimmers David Wilkie, Nick Gillingham and Tim Jones at a promotional event at Ladywood Baths. They made a splash about healthy lifestyles and went to grrrreat lengths to promote healthy eating. Abid, Leroy, Tricia and Michelle from St John's School joined in the fun.

Star swimmer at Ladywood Baths and Olympic medallist Nick Gillingham shows off Ladywood School's newspaper, while Brendan Brogan shows off his Olympic medal. This was taken in front of Ladywood School in an area once covered by the back-to-back houses on Beach Street. Leach Street ran next to it before Icknield Square was reached. Part of the square still exists and can be seen in the background of this photograph. The taller buildings at the rear belonged to Belliss & Morcom.

One of a series of photographs which were taken of the demolition of the baths in 1994. (*Eileen Doyle*)

Members of the Birmingham Deaf Club in Granville Street perform a play as part of a Christmas pantomime in 1933.

A postcard of Osler Athletic FC, 1922/3. This was possibly formed by old boys of the school. A handwritten message on the back of it reads, 'Bernard next to Harry Bagley, Horace and Belly (?) and Fred Rogers. You will know a lot of faces.'

Swan Athletic FC, 1938. This team was based at the pub on the corner of King Edward's Road and Stour Street. Back row, left to right: J. Gibbons, L. Prince, F. Haywood (coach driver), L. Strawford, S. Lewis (licensee). Middle row: B. Harris, G. Wakefield, ? Dawson, G. Griffin, B. Portman, -?-, A. Markham. Front row: W. Mitchell, F. Gibbons, S. Gibbons, H. Balman, C. Gibbons, G. Harris, B. Williams, F. Ventham.

The 4th Birmingham Boys' Brigade Cricket Champions, 1948. Back row, left to right: Len Bryan, Ralph Hickman, 'Hockey' Strawford, Vernon Thomas, Phillip Plummer, Frank Spencer. Front row: Ken Sheen, Ronnie Bryan, Kenny Powell, Roy Tompkins, Harry Bennett.

Christ Church Summerfield FC, 1944. Len Ward recalls: 'Most of the players were from Ladywood. I'm the one in the centre – the small lad on the floor with the ball. Canon Hinnett is also on the picture. The team was founded in 1927. When this was taken we were one of the best teams in the district and we won quite a few cups. Christ Church FC became Chelmsley Town FC and I am now their Vice President.' (*Len Ward*)

The cup winning side from Aluminium Die Castings FC, 1961/2. Back row, left to right: Dave Morris, Manus Moran, M. Hall, Frank Bagnall, Alfred Kettle, Barry McLaren. Front row: Eddie Johnson, Mickey Michell, Johnnie Downing, Robert Cunningham, Johnnie McLaren.

While brewers claimed to be brewing 'For the Men of the Midlands', the women behind the men also got up a thirst and knew how to celebrate. The supporters of the Brew XI team of the Pied Piper pub in Ledsam Street in June 1972 are, left to right: -?-, Nicky Howells, Mary Green, Janet Cunningham, Sadie Cunningham, Margaret Rogerson, Bridie Cunningham, P. Harrington, Diane Kelly. Diane is mother to David Kelly, who became a fine professional footballer.

The Sunday Alliance League Division One with all the trophies they won in the 1972 season. Back row, left to right: J. Cunningham, B. Cunningham, T. Sullivan, T. Cunningham, R. Green, B. Loughran, N. Howells. Front row: G. Quirke, F. Poole, R. McCulloch, -?-, W. Quirke, R. Kelly.

The Edgbaston Assembly Rooms, which were at the junction of Hagley Road and Francis Road, July 1958. Behind lies the Edgbaston Congregational church. The road was built on land owned by a Mr Francis and the church was built on land purchased from him for just over £1,500 in 1854.

Lloyd's Rhythmic Dance Band, which was based at the Edgbaston Assembly Rooms in Francis Road. This is an advertising postcard for the group. The reverse informs us that they played at the Assembly Rooms every Monday and Wednesday, 7.30 p.m. to 11.00 p.m. Admission was 3s. They also played at the Queen's College on Paradise Street for 2s 6d on Saturday nights.

Winners of the Midland Deaf Sports Association Billiards and Snooker competition in 1975 pictured at their Ladywood Road Social Club.

The Lyric Cinema, August 1957. The billboards advertise *Wings of an Eagle* and Burt Lancaster in *Crimson Pirate*. The Morris van is parked on Edward Street and the road along the side of the building is Helena Street. This cinema was originally a church built for George Dawson, called the Church of the Saviour. It became a cinema in about 1919 and closed at the end of the 1950s.

The Reservoir pub at the corner of Osler Street and Reservoir Road, 25 October 1965. The Silver Birch lounge is on the Osler Street side and the sign above the lady on the Reservoir Road side reads 'Lakeside' and 'Offsales'. The landlord's name above the door reads Stanley Daniel Downing. Customers could well be celebrating West Brom's 3–0 thrashing of Liverpool, with goals from Brown, Kaye and Clark. Cheers!

The Burton Stores on The Parade, 31 July 1963. The pub and the adjacent occupants, Pearsall the butcher and the medical herbal stores, had all been on this site since at least 1872. The people here were probably discussing the big football news that Tony Hateley had been transferred from Notts County to Aston Villa.

The Beehive pub on Garbett Street as it looked in 1964. The pub stands in splendid isolation, as all of the buildings around it had been demolished to make way for the new look Ladywood. Frank Walters says: 'The car is a Vauxhall Victor which belonged to my brother. I took this photograph when standing on top of a pile of bricks from demolished houses across the road.' (*Frank Walters*)

The Roebuck pub at the corner of Belliss Street and Monument Road, December 1972. The adjacent tobacconist is run by George Snape. His snowy windows behind the Unigate milk float are a sure sign that Christmas was fast approaching. (*Birmingham City Council collection*)

The Eagle Tavern on the corner of Oozells Street North and Oozells Street. The large factory in the background is the Wale's Atlas Works bed manufactory which was featured in the first volume of *Ladywood in Old Photographs*. Both factory and pub were derelict at the time this was taken in 1986.

Outside the Eagle Tavern on Oozells Street North, *c.* 1935. George Elmer says: 'I don't remember this being taken because I was only four at the time, but I know my mother is on it. She is in the middle of the crowd standing behind the large boy who has his hands in his pockets at the front. Mom's name was Jane and she worked as a core maker at Hunt & Mitton's which was just up the street. This was probably a day out organised by the pub. Other people on it include Mrs Firkin, Kate Gregory, Lil Purchase and Floss Parry.' (*George Elmer*)

The Five Ways Inn at the corner of Broad Street and Ladywood Road, 1 July 1959. This scene was totally transformed once the pub was demolished in about 1965 for the building of the Five Ways island and Tesco. On the Broad Street side notice the distinctive barber's pole belonging to Gough the hairdresser. Next door stood the long established Crowe's newsagent.

The White Swan on Grosvenor Street West, December 1987.

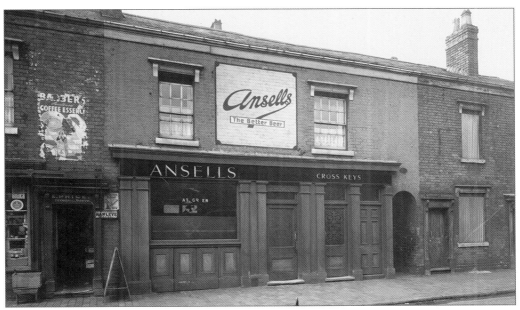

The Cross Keys on Steward Street, 1 April 1954. Some of the lettering on the window can be seen and made to spell 'Watty Green'. John Landon says: 'My dad used to live up the entry on the right and my gran used to sell faggots and peas outside the pub on Friday and Saturday nights!' (*John Landon*)

The Summerhill Tavern was built in 1899. It was particularly popular with skaters visiting the ice rink which was almost opposite the front door. (*Birmingham City Council collection*)

The Steam Clock on Morville Street.

The Mint on Icknield Street. This pub was popular with boxers from the Mint's boxing club, clearly a place to have a few 'rounds' after going a few 'rounds'!

A day trip for the workers at Parker Winder Achurch, *c.* 1930. At the time PWA was based on Broad Street near Oozells Street Church. In 1936 they moved across the road where they remained until 1972.

Staff from Syke's timber yard in Sheepcote Street on their annual works outing to Great Yarmouth, 1898. It appears they may have stayed in the Pier Hotel.

An outing to an unknown destination from the Oratory, probably mid-1920s.

The 36th Birmingham Boy's Brigade on the way to camp at Holyhead, 1959 or 1960. Albert Mousdale, who is on the second row on the left, said: 'These camps were always brilliant and it was the only holiday that many of us had. I know the first one that I went on in 1957 only cost £4 15s. We went rambling, swimming, and played all kinds of sports, but kept the discipline of the parade and inspections. Some kids from another company are with us. The boys include Robert Kirby, Billy Behan, Terry Gardner, Peter Carling and Laurence and David Houston.' (*Albert Mousdale*)

Boys' Brigade member Albert Mousdale, on the left, was thirteen when this photograph was taken in 1960. He is with friend and fellow drummer Graham Bird at the Summerhill Methodist church hall. (*Albert Mousdale*)

The 4th Birmingham Boys' Brigade at Burnham on Sea, 1947. Members on the back row include Frank Spencer, Ken Sheen, Evan Morris, Roy Tomkins, Ken Powell, Ron Bryan, Ralph Hickman, Joe Hoskins. The middle row includes Gordon Cull, Len Bryan, Roy Smith. The front lads include John 'Clem' Spencer, Fred Gauder, Eddie Wheeler and John Sheen.

A well-disciplined group from the 4th Birmingham Boys' Brigade ready for inspection at Harlech in 1946. Most of the boys, including Gordon Cull and Ken Wheeler, were from Ladywood even though they met at the Church of the Redeemer.

The Boys' Brigade march from their home church, the Church of the Redeemer on the junction of Hagley Road and Wyndham Road. (*Ken Strangward*)

5

Events & Happenings

Jubilee celebrations in Osler Street, 1935.

Closed school on Thursday *at. 31. 3*
(24th inst.) to allow teachers to hear
Proclamation of King Edward VII.
School resumed as usual in the
afternoon   Attendance Good

January 28th to Feb 1st 1901.

"School closed on Friday.=
"Funeral of our dear & beloved
Queen Victoria"

The proclamation of King Edward VII and the funeral of Queen Victoria as it is recorded in the log book at Brookfield's Infants School, January 1901.

A postcard showing the celebrations in Summerfield Park to mark the seventieth birthday of Joseph Chamberlain on 8 July 1906. The text on the back reads: 'This is "Joey" at one of the parks. There was some people about on that day.' Three days after this event he suffered the stroke which ended his active political life. He died in 1914. The government offered a Westminster Abbey funeral, but his family decided it would be better for him to be buried among his own people. Many thousands of people lined the streets as his cortège travelled from his home at Highbury Hall in Moseley to Key Hill cemetery.

CITY OF BIRMINGHAM.

... Visit of ...

Their Majesties The King and Queen

21st MAY, 1919.

Admit Bearer, with Company of Girl Guides, to reserved enclosure from Five Ways to opposite Grosvenor Street West (West Side).

To be in position, 9 a.m., sharp

DAVID BROOKS,
Lord Mayor.

One of the tickets issued to the Girl Guides to enable them to assemble to see the King and Queen in 1919. They were in Ladywood to visit the Children's Hospital on Ladywood Road.

The world-renowned hospital was officially called the King Edward VII Memorial Hospital. It was visited by King George V and Queen Mary on 21 May 1919. The royal couple later held an Investiture and visited the Bournville Model Village. The Princess Louise, Duchess of Argyll, laid the hospital's foundation stone in April 1913. (*Victor Price*)

Seven-year-old Janet Taylor of Anderton Street at the Children's Hospital. She says: 'I was one of the first children to undergo pioneering heart surgery at the hospital in May 1947. The operation was performed by Professor Alphonsus Ligurid Abreu. I kept in touch with him for many years after the operation.' (*Janet Beale, née Taylor*)

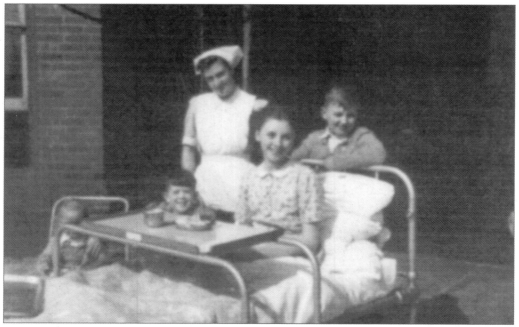

Janet recuperates in the summer sunshine at the Children's Hospital. She said: 'When it was nice weather the nurses opened the large glass and wood doors and pushed out some of the beds.'

A Sunday School anniversary day out from Christ Church in Marroway Street, *c.* 1926. Len Ward recalls: 'We all dressed up in our finest clothes and had an unofficial competition to see who could get dressed up the best. We always did this on the church's anniversary and we marched with a band and banners to Summerfield Crescent and along Icknield Port Road, Coplow Street and Marroway Street and back to the church. Bertram Ward is the lad who is holding the card on the extreme right of the photograph.' (*Len Ward*)

The Oratory Church Benediction Parade, *c.* 1930. The houses in the background are on Plough and Harrow Road.

Band 16th Service R.W.R.

The band of the 16th Service of the Royal Warwickshire Regiment at Malvern prior to setting off for the First World War. The proud soldier at the front is Sergeant Drummer Frank Grigg of Morville Street. He was a compositor for James Upton printers in Cambridge Street. Like so many others he was wounded in the trenches, but luckily survived and returned to work for Upton's for a total of fifty years.

A typical 1920s wedding. This one was held at the Methodist chapel on Monument Road almost opposite the Dispensary. Joan Jones says: 'This is my mother and father at their wedding in 1924. My father, Arnold, worked on the railways and my mother Winifred worked with the WRVS.' (*Joan Jones née Morton*)

Food glorious food for the residents of Osler Street as they celebrate the Silver Jubilee of King George and Queen Mary, May 1935. The celebrations across the city saw the biggest crowds out on the streets since Armistice Day in 1918 (*Frank Hunt*)

Jubilee celebrations in Osler Street, 1935. Mrs Crisp is holding the flag and either side of her are Mr Neale and Mrs Parry. Those behind them are other residents of the street, who include Elsie Dorset, Billy Dorset, Mr Mullet, Mr Grinsell, Florrie Howell, Mrs Beavan, Mrs Reynolds and Frankie Parry. (*Frank Hunt*)

Boys and girls in party mood in Osler Street. This was also probably part of the Jubilee celebrations in 1935. (*Frank Hunt*)

Again we cannot be 100 per cent certain, but this is also likely to be the 1935 Jubilee celebrations. It is definitely in Icknield Square. The road across the top is Monument Road and the big building at the junction is Fulwood's, which sold men's clothes and shoes. (*Irene Adams née Parkes*)

Another scene of celebration. This was a Coronation party in 1953, which was held in Summerfield Crescent. The people on the photograph include Anna, Gordon, Lucy and Rita Cull, May Hogarth and Alan and Rose Thorp.

Coronation day, June 1953. A mystery street – the only clue, apart from the people, being the sweet shop on the right. Any suggestions as to where it may be?

The Coronation party in honour of George VI as it was celebrated in Anderton Street, 1937. The lad on the right with the cap is Ernie Pearce. Leslie Checkley says: 'Although this was a special event we often had similar type parties at weekends. On Saturday nights someone would wheel a piano down the street to a neighbour's house and we'd all have a sing song!' (*Leslie Checkley*)

Tough times in the winter of 1947. Here a supply of wood has been delivered and is eagerly collected by Ladywood residents from outside St John's School on St Mary Street at the junction of Johnstone Street. (*Anthony Spettigue*)

Back to 1937 and the Coronation of King George VI. This was taken in Steward Street outside the Cross Keys pub. Rene Landon, of the well-known bathroom family, is on the immediate left with the headband. This was the first Coronation at which the BBC did an outside broadcast of a procession, but it is likely that no one in Ladywood would have known about it. The next Coronation in 1953 caused a rush of people to buy televisions, and families crushed into neighbours' homes to watch it. Street parties like this one would never be the same again! (*John Landon*)

Cadets from TS *Vernon* under extensive training as part of the war effort in 1944. This photograph was taken on the canal just up from Sheepcote Street Bridge looking towards the city centre. The shed in the background has now been replaced by the car parks and walkway of the National Indoor Arena. (*TS* Vernon *archive*)

During the Second World War many schoolchildren were evacuated to rural Herefordshire and Wales. Many returned to Ladywood within a few weeks, but others stayed. This group were from Osler Street School and they attended the Burghill School in Hereford. The class was made up of half of Osler Street and half local children. The teacher is Miss Dyer from Osler Street Senior Girls' School. (*Gordon Cull*)

At the Town Hall in 1944 or 1945, when the King and Queen visited to thank and 'gee-up' the children of the city. Naturally, Ladywood children made sure they got the best seats! Right behind the royal couple at the front of the balcony are the head boy and girl from the Osler Street schools, Gordon Cull and Greeta Crawford. Behind them is the school captain from St Barnabas School in Ryland Street.

A wartime wedding of Lillian Fisher and Micahel Carleton at the Oratory Church, 1942.

The Mothers' Union at St John's Church, 1942. Joan Jones says: 'My mother Winifred Morton is on the back row, eighth from left, my grandmother Fanny Taylor is on the front row, third left and my brother Kenneth is one of those who is sitting at the front.' (*Joan Jones née Morton*)

This is obviously a celebration, but the mystery is what is being celebrated? The photograph was taken in Rann Street. Maybe the coach was taking the children off to a large event to celebrate the Coronation in 1953. (*Ken Strangward*)

The 1953 Coronation as it was celebrated on Icknield Port Road.

The 1953 Coronation as it was celebrated in part of Beach Street. Two of the girls are Marie and Patty Hollins. (*George Thorp*)

The 1953 Coronation celebrations at the Ice Rink. Ida Russell says: 'I was one of a team of sixteen girls who performed and marched in formation to the tune from "Top of the Form". Eileen Hartung arranged the event. My costume was an ordinary white skating dress with a red sash. It was a great occasion, but fewer people than we expected turned up to watch us. We think many people were watching the events on television.' (*Ida Russell*)

Neighbours celebrate the 1953 Coronation in Beach Street. Pictured are Mrs Spencer and Mary Fisher. (*Lindy Dunnett née Carleton*)

A special day for railway enthusiasts at Monument Lane station, June 1950. This was the last passenger-carrying special to run on the line. (*Roger Carpenter*)

A party in progress at Osler Street School, *c.* 1950. It would appear to be a Christmas party, but as many adults are there it is likely that it was an event for the local residents rather than a class party. (Gordon Cull)

Police show off their latest in high speed bikes in Summerfield Park. (*West Midlands Police Museum*)

'Evening all. Over. . . .' Police, again in Summerfield Park, try out their new A60 radio car. (*West Midlands Police Museum*)

The *Sunday Mercury* newspaper held an annual 'Mercury Girl' contest for the people of the Midlands. A Ladywood girl, Joan Taylor of Anderton Street, won through to the final after reaching the area final of the competition. Each entrant sent in a photograph and the judges selected the contestants from all the pictures received.

Joan Taylor's gran Emily is pictured with the sash. Joan says: 'I was a runner up in the final of 1956. It was a grand exciting evening. I was presented with an engraved powder compact, which I still have. The winning girl won a cheque for £250. We took the photograph of my gran wearing the sash and holding my bouquet of flowers. It was given to me when I was chosen to go forward to the area final.' (*Joan Reeves née Taylor*)

The Royal Wedding of 1981. Prince Charles and Lady Diana's wedding was celebrated with a big party at Ladywood Community Centre on St Vincent Street. Seated at the front is Gill Robinson. At the time of writing Gill is Chairman of the Ladywood Neighbourhood Forum.

The celebrations to commemorate the Royal Wedding of 1981 continued into the afternoon. The pub in the background is the Saint Vincent.

Four of the staff at Ladywood Community Centre, 1975. They are Francis Curtis, Nell Bailey, Doris Hines and Dorothy Williams. Truro Tower on the left and Ledbury Close look remarkably clean and litter free!

The opening of the Ladywood Health & Community Centre, by Winnie Horton, with pupils from local schools. (See page 139)

The Ladywood Community Forum organised a Clean Up Ladywood campaign in 1989. There was a massive show of support from pupils from local schools and residents of the area. Here a group from Ladywood School are seen with the results of their work on Chamberlain Gardens estate.

A photograph taken to publicise the Clean Up. Pam Edwards, chairman of the Community Forum, proves she's as daft as a brush as she sweeps aside two pupils from Ladywood School!

Three members of the WRVS, Mrs Stanton, Miss Horton and Mrs Morton. Winnie ran the WVS Darby & Joan Club for many years, first in Coplow Street then at The Beeches and now at St John's Church hall. She was an auxiliary nurse during the Second World War. As part of her voluntary work she set up Birmingham's first luncheon club. Winnie's father was a well-known local coal merchant.

Winnie was named in John Major's first 'classless' New Year's honours list in December 1993 and received an MBE for her forty years of voluntary work. She is pictured outside Buckingham Palace with her MBE and friends Ede Ockford and Stewart and Edna Collins. (*Ede Ockford*)

The opening of the Birmingham Institute for the Deaf's new premises on Ladywood Road in 1974. Eric Ashton, Leslie Wickens, Chair of the project committee, the Bishop of Birmingham, the Right Revd Laurence Brown, the Lord Mayor, Councillor Marjorie Brown, Michael Raine, Chairman of BID and Mrs Laurence Brown. (*BID Archives*)

A beer lorry crashed into this shop on the corner of Icknield Port Road and Dudley Road in the summer of 1988. Luckily, no one was seriously injured. The shop was called Bits & Pieces!

Prince Charles visited Birmingham in 1991 and stopped off at Ladywood Arts & Leisure Centre where he saw the work of the Prince's Trust. During his visit he was presented with this cake to mark his fortieth birthday.

The statue of Blondin, which now stands on Ladywood Middleway, under construction. Blondin once walked across Edgbaston Reservoir on a tightrope, calling it the great divide. Today the Middleway is seen as the great divide cutting Ladywood in two.

In 1999 two stained glass windows were erected in St John's Church by an artist who worked to designs drawn up by local residents. One was dedicated to the memory of churchwarden Jean Whitburn and shows scenes of Ladywood. The other is a Caribbean window depicting scenes from the islands. Pictured at the unveiling are Brian Whitburn with his son Steve and grandson Thomas.

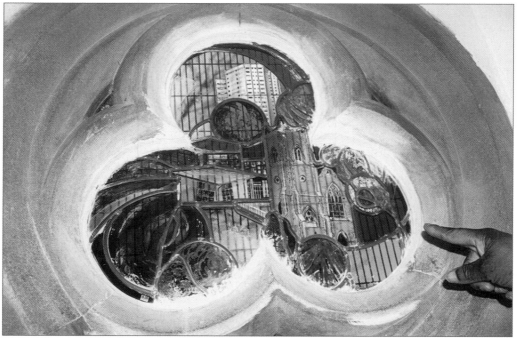

The Ladywood window at St John's Church in more detail. Look out for the tower blocks, St John's Church, St John's School, Ladywood Middleway and Edgbaston Reservoir.

6

Rebuilding Ladywood

The Ladywood Middleway cuts its way through Ladywood, July 1971. The new shops at the corner of the newly truncated King Edward's Road are in the bottom left corner. Ladywood School is under construction at the top left.

Work in progress to build the Five Ways island and underpass, September 1970. The Assembly Rooms at the corner of Francis Road and Hagley Road are about to be demolished. This is the building on page 105. (*Birmingham City Council collection*)

The bridge over the canal on Monument Road is widened to become Ladywood Middleway. Presumably, the bridge wall would have been in the middle of the road had it not been demolished. Appropriately enough, the band Middle of the Road had been top of the charts that summer with 'Chirpy, Chirpy, Cheep, Cheep'. The construction of the road certainly didn't come cheap! This was taken in November 1971. (*Birmingham City Council collection*)

St Barnabas School on Ryland Street, August 1964. A report in 1949 found the boundary wall was 'bulging under the pressure of weight and heat from the adjacent factory buildings'. At the bottom of the road stands the three-year-old St John's School on St Vincent Street. The view to it was made possible thanks to the demolition of Morville Street, Blythe Street and Friston Street. Soon the buildings on Ryland Street would suffer a similar fate.

An emergency in Browning Street. Jim Taylor remembers: 'This was taken from an attic window in Browning Street during the demolition of the houses in 1964. A lorry which had arrived to collect the rubble was driven on to the site. Unfortunately, it seems no one told the driver about the cellars which lay underground. Presumably the floor on one of them gave way under the weight of the lorry and it fell into the cellar.' (*Jim Taylor*)

St John's School is under construction in this view, which was taken in August 1960. The shops on the right are at the corner of Ledsam Street and St Vincent Street. The fencing in the foreground marks a path along the line of the old Sherborne Street. (*David Smith*)

The last remaining houses on Wood Street are demolished and the new ones are under construction. This is the new Holywell Close and Sadlers Walk development. (*Victor Price*)

Allensmoor House was built off Great Tindal Street at the end of the 1950s. It was a six-storey block of flats and maisonettes which soon became unpopular with residents, because of heating and ventilation problems and poor security. It is pictured here in 1986. Ploughfield House, a similar block, is in the background. That too was demolished and Ladywood Neighbourhood Office was built in their place. (*David Smith*)

Hereford House on Ledsam Street on the left was similar to the blocks pictured above and was demolished in 1986. The terrace next door was once the same as Hereford House, but the top storeys were lopped off and the remains converted into houses.

The author's nan Mrs Wilson with one of her daughters Kathleen. Nan lived in St Mark's Street and later in the flats on the previous page before moving into the top-lopped homes when they were completed in 1986.

In the early 1960s things were changing fast. Harold Wilson became leader of the Labour party, Cliff Richard's *Summer Holiday* premiered in London and the country had its coldest January since 1740. The outlook was cold and bleak in this view from March 1963 of the pathway which was all that was left of the now truncated Ledsam Street. The new tower block, called Lincoln Tower, dominates the view with the remaining old houses on Morville Street awaiting demolition.

An aerial view from Truro Tower looking along St Vincent Street West to St John's School. The tallest block on the left is Blythe Tower, named after Blythe Street which disappeared during redevelopment. Blythe House was also soon to disappear.

Blythe House was replaced by Victoria House, a development which was opened by Baroness Fisher who was MP for Ladywood in 1974. She is pictured with many of the elderly residents, holding a bouquet.

Victoria House as it looked when it first opened. The tower block behind it, Blythe Tower, is awaiting demolition.

Two residents of Victoria House, Mary Martin on the left and Ede Ockford, with fellow lifelong Ladywood resident Myra Curley, local historian Carl Chinn and a certain book about Ladywood. The three ladies spoke on Carl's BBC Radio WM show about old Ladywood and the book.

Open space was at a premium in old Ladywood and even when the redevelopment had taken place the amount of play space was limited. Much of the open land was either on a slope or had bushes on it, or was too near houses for children to play sports such as football. Often, any flat land had the 'no ball games here' sign on it. In this photograph children play football on the drive of St John's Church. (*John Landon*)

Play areas were built when Ladywood was redeveloped and at first they proved popular, but as children grew up and became more sophisticated the play areas held less appeal. A cold, metal slide could be made more fun if you used your loaf and slid down on a greasy bread wrapper! There was little appeal in balancing across a dead tree, but you needed to be alert in case you fell off on to the hard surface below. Television was also seriously beginning to affect playtime. BBC2 began broadcasting in the month this photograph was taken in April 1964.

St John's School is under construction in this view of the new Gilby Road estate. The children's play area is in the bottom left corner.

A close-up view of the Gilby Road play area. A certain train of thought suggests these play areas were not designed very well! As far as the children were concerned the concrete ship certainly didn't go down as well as the *Titanic*.

A view from a balcony in June 1992 looking into the interior of the now demolished Gilby Road estate. Ladywood Middleway runs across the photograph behind the block. Ladywood police station can be seen behind the trees.

Cavell House, the last of the Gilby Road flats, is in the process of demolition in October 1997. The newly built houses prepare for their occupants in this view from Ladywood Middleway. The redesigned estate was opened by local MP Clare Short.

The remains of St John's Infants School and the caretaker's house at the junction of Johnstone Street and St Mary's Street, July 1967. The new estate is springing up behind it. Johnstone Street has now disappeared altogether except for a few yards in front of Wells Tower. The end building on the right is 61 Guild Close. This is where, in early 1966, Mandy Winward, now Mrs Slammon, moved. She recalls: 'We moved into this new, bigger house from our old home on Essington Street. This had underfloor heating which turned out to be very expensive, but it was quite new and posh at the time! When the school was being demolished the area was plagued by rats. I was about four years old when we opened the front door and a huge rat was in the porch area. I remember my mom tried to hit it with a tea towel but it ran off!' (*John Landon*)

The new St John's School as it looked in April 1962. This was taken from the grassed area at the rear of the school, which was once the line of Friston Street.

These homes were erected in the mid-1950s on Ryland Street, near to the junction with Broad Street. This picture was taken in about 1990. The one below is the same view as it looks today.

The homes pictured above were renovated in the 1990s. Externally, it is noticeable that the window balconies were altered and the stairwells were enclosed for extra safety. The office block on the corner is on Broad Street.

The old and the new sit side by side. The horseshoe-shaped stables remain to this day. They were built to stable horses which were used to transport goods delivered by canal and railway. Across the road from the main entrance stands an elderly persons' home on the site of the former flour mill. To the left stands a development of houses known as the Kilby Lighthorne Estate, built across what was once extensive railway marshalling yards. Anyone who has recently walked along the stretch of canal will have noticed the way that Ladywood is changing. The factories on the lower right have been demolished and a major housing complex is being built. A penthouse suite is expected to sell for £1 million! The factories on the lower left, between the canal and Browning Street, will be demolished by the end of 2001; these too will be replaced by upmarket residential accommodation.

The building at the junction to the right of the stables is the former British Railways Working Men's Club. This has now been demolished and is being replaced by yet more accommodation. A plan to build a railway station, near the play area at the top of the picture, hit the buffers in spring 2001. At least the stables building remains relatively unaltered and it is now a craft centre and successful pub called the Fiddle and 'Bone.

A final new chapter in the history of Spring Hill Library was almost written in the early 1970s, when the planners' script almost led to the demolition of the building. A redrafting of the plans, following a public outcry, resulted in a reprieve and the new road was built around the building rather than through it! Traffic congestion became an increasing problem. A survey in 1988 showed that at peak time over 1,200 vehicles passed along Summerhill towards the city centre. It was predicted that the figures would increase once the International Convention Centre was open. In an attempt to prevent this junction becoming a bottleneck, a traffic island was built. Work is under way to build the island in this photograph and the magnificent library remained, continuing to dominate the scene.

The library is not so dominant when viewed from the top of Durham Tower. Another block, Canterbury Tower, reaches for the sky. Buildings have changed and so has society. In 1895 a man was sentenced to six weeks' imprisonment with hard labour for the 'blackguardly conduct' of throwing books around the library and resisting arrest!

On Francis Road work is in progress to demolish the Children's Hospital and nurses' home to make way for an entertainment complex consisting of a twenty screen cinema, twenty lane bowling alley and shops and restaurants. This will be known as Broadway Plaza and the publicity machine says it will be 'the talking point of Europe'. It's certainly the talking point of Ladywood, as in 'not more cinema screens. They've just opened a cinema on the other side of Five Ways, so why do we need more?' Who will be proved correct?

The front of the Children's Hospital building is overshadowed as work continues on Broadway Plaza. The façade of the building will be incorporated into the new development. The people in the adjacent almshouses will at least have something to do at night!

Ladywood as it looked in the last decade of the twentieth century. Ladywood Middleway cuts across the bottom third of this photograph and turns up the left-hand side. St John's Church, one of the few remaining buildings of old Ladywood, is next to the large traffic island. Monument Road, once one of the great roads of the city, leads down from the island and off the photograph to the Ivy Bush junction with Hagley Road. St Vincent Street runs up the centre of the photograph leading to the spaceship-shaped National Indoor Arena. Below that lie central Ladywood's tower blocks. The open space has appeared because of the demolition of most of the Gilby Road area flats; some are still to be demolished. The Chamberlain Gardens estate lies in the bottom right-hand corner. The remains of Ladywood Road form the third side of a triangle from Monument Road towards Ladywood Middleway. (*Brindleyplace archives*)

STREET NAMES INDEX